*Should You Marry Him? A No-Nonsense,
Therapist-Tested Guide to Not Screwing Up the
Biggest Decision of Your Life* will help you:

- Assess the quality of your love relationship
- Learn why minimizing the importance of sex can be fatal to your relationship
- Consider commonly overlooked lifestyle issues that can derail your marriage
- Understand why the "kid decision" is so crucial
- Recognize why hurting each other can be healing
- Identify why making changes for your relationship may not be healthiest option in the long run
- Answer the one critical question you must ask yourself *before* you say yes

Should You Marry Him?

A NO-NONSENSE, THERAPIST-TESTED* GUIDE TO NOT
SCREWING UP THE BIGGEST DECISION OF YOUR LIFE

ABBY RODMAN, LICSW*

BALBOA.
PRESS
A DIVISION OF HAY HOUSE

Balboa Press books may be ordered through booksellers or by contacting:

Balboa Press
A Division of Hay House
1663 Liberty Drive
Bloomington, IN 47403
www.balboapress.com
1 (877) 407-4847

Because of the dynamic nature of the Internet, any web addresses or links contained
in this book may have changed since publication and may no longer be valid. The views
expressed in this work are solely those of the author and do not necessarily reflect the
views of the publisher, and the publisher hereby disclaims any responsibility for them.

Every effort has been made to protect the privacy of individuals
in the writing of this book. Any resemblance to actual persons,
living or dead, or actual events is purely coincidental.

If expert assistance or counseling is needed, the services of a trained
professional should be sought. Any application of the material in the
following pages is at the reader's discretion and sole responsibility.

The author of this book does not dispense medical advice or prescribe the use
of any technique as a form of treatment for physical, emotional, or medical
problems without the advice of a physician, either directly or indirectly. The
intent of the author is only to offer information of a general nature to help you
in your quest for emotional and spiritual well-being. In the event you use any
of the information in this book for yourself, which is your constitutional right,
the author and the publisher assume no responsibility for your actions.

Any people depicted in stock imagery provided by Thinkstock are models,
and such images are being used for illustrative purposes only.
Certain stock imagery © Thinkstock.

Printed in the United States of America.

ISBN: 978-1-4525-8729-5 (sc)
ISBN: 978-1-4525-8730-1 (e)
Library of Congress Control Number: 2013921196

Balboa Press rev. date: 12/18/2013

CONTENTS

INTRODUCTION _____ ix

Chapter One
IS IT LOVE? _____ I

Chapter Two
HOW'S THE SEX? _____ 5

Chapter Three
ARE YOU LOVED 'AS IS'? _____ I I

Chapter Four
WANT KIDS? _____ 17

Chapter Five
TELL ME WHERE IT HURTS _____ 23

Chapter Six
FILL IN YOUR OWN BLANKS _____ 29

Chapter Seven
FIGHTING AND FORGIVING _____ 35

Chapter Eight

ADULTERY, ADDICTION AND ABUSE_____41

Chapter Nine

THEIRS AND OURS: MAKING YOUR MARRIAGE
    YOUR OWN_____53

Chapter Ten

ANSWER THIS QUESTION OR FOREVER HOLD
    YOUR PEACE_____59

I do.

Very few words, if any, have the power to change your life as exponentially as those two.

Whether you're already planning the wedding or just considering his proposal, know that you are in the process of making the most important decision of your life. Sound daunting? A little scary, even? Good. That means you're truly considering what it will mean to be *married* to this man. You're thinking about what's at stake in choosing him, forsaking all others, to be your companion, mate and lover through your one, precious life.

You know those movies in which the hero wakes up one day and finds he's the only man left on Earth? Then, miraculously, he finds the one woman left on the planet living in some bombed-out apartment building? And, lucky for him, through all the dirt and torn clothing he can see she's the hottest chick ever? And initially they hate each other but realize they really love each other and decide to begin their task of rebuilding the human race?

Okay, maybe getting married isn't *that* dramatic but it's not far from it. Either you choose the right partner to help you successfully navigate this strange, new world called Marriage or you choose the wrong one and begin your descent into unhappy-marriage hell.

With your "I do", you will mark the start of the rest of your life. Your new husband will be the last man you'll ever have a first date with, the last man you ever French kiss, the last man you'll ever share a bed with. This man will be the father of your children and that's an irreversible choice. You'll slog through the everyday routine that is life and, if you're lucky, that life will also be peppered with joy and moments of passion that make you both sigh and remember the good old days of coat closet sex.

You will know this man, if all goes well, better than you have ever known another person. You will share his fears, his moments of glory and his bathroom. You'll also become expert at reading his moods, accepting his limitations and soothing his demons. Yes, he has demons. We all do. And if you haven't seen your man's yet, you will. Make no mistake.

No matter how you slice it, marriage is a gamble. Statistics vary but somewhere in the neighborhood of 40 to 50 percent of first marriages end in divorce. Let's put it this way: Nearly half of you reading this book will get divorced. And if the numbers are that high for people who make the difficult decision to split, how many couples stay married and miserable? My clinical guesstimate is that you have about a 25 percent chance of ending up in happy marriage. Sweating, yet?

Perhaps you think of divorce as something that happens to other people. If that's true, next time you have dinner with your three closest girlfriends, take a look around the table. In time, two of you will be divorced from your spouses. Although the high rate of divorce has yet to dissuade folks from marrying, it hasn't made the experience of divorce any easier. Ask anyone who has gone through it and you'll hear the same descriptions of anger, grief and disillusionment.

I'm a psychotherapist who has worked with hundreds of couples. I'm also divorced. I offer here what I've learned from my own experience and from those clients who have trusted me with the morass of their marriages. Whether you're euphorically in love and happily planning your nuptials or you're reading this book because you're not sure, please don't put it down. You owe it to yourself (and to your man) to at least consider what's in it.

Too many times I've heard clients say they knew something just wasn't right even as they walked down the aisle. Lorena, now 48 and divorced, points to her wedding ceremony tears two decades ago as proof she was conflicted even as she said her vows. Like so many others, she felt that once she got aboard the runaway train also known as planning a wedding, there was no easy way to get off. Lorena got swept up in the frenzy of carats, caterers and cakes, and overlooked the warning signs that she was headed into a stormy union.

There's no question that planning and executing (hmm, interesting word choice) a wedding can be both fun and meaningful. If you choose, your wedding day may be nothing short of a Disney extravaganza. For one day, you'll be dressed up like a fairy princess and your bridegroom like the butler on Downton Abbey. Flower petals will be scattered where you walk. A royal court will attend to your dress, hair, and makeup. Hired help will scurry like scared rabbits to do your bidding. For a whole day, loving paparazzi will photograph your every move.

In other words, it's nothing remotely like the real life that's to follow. Sadly, too many brides focus more on their wedding day details than the 50-year marriage to come.

When my children were younger, I heard an older mom's desperation in her desire that her teenage daughters would eventually marry the right men. "Who they marry will determine whether or not the rest of their lives are happy," she bemoaned. I dismissed her feelings then as irrational angst. Now, I see the wisdom in her words.

No other relationship in your life will provide you more

happiness or pain, companionship or loneliness, security or fear. No other person will ever have the private access to you that your husband will. What happens behind your front door will remain a mystery to others despite how well they know and love you. No one, *but no one*, knows what goes on in a marriage except for the two people in it. That's what makes a good marriage so healthy and a bad one so scary.

Healthy, loving, successful marriages do exist. We can all name a couple or two we admire for their devotion and perseverance. But you can be sure those very same couples have struggled to keep their marriages intact. The same issue that makes one couple split and another stronger will forever mystify me in my work. That's why comparing your relationship to someone else's is a fool's errand. It won't get you anywhere.

As I tell my clients, each and every couple cuts their own deal. Those couples who make it when confronted with challenges (and you *will* be confronted with challenges) are usually those who asked themselves the tough questions before they married.

That's the purpose of this book - to get you to analyze core issues in your relationship before you say yes to the dress, choose your bridesmaids, and spend a lot of people's hard earned money. Oh, yes, and that not-so-small detail of pledging your life to this man. Don't be afraid. It's okay if your relationship isn't perfect. No relationship is. But you must be willing to trust your gut. No one gets married thinking she will get divorced, but almost half of us do. The odds are near even but it's no casual bet.

I have spent many years studying the relationship patterns of couples, gay and straight, in both monogamous and open relationships, and every variation in between. Consistent themes reliably appear and reappear for those struggling in their marriages. In this book, I've compiled a list of the ten make-or-break pre-marriage issues I see on a near-daily basis. One or more of these issues pop up in every troubled relationship I've been privy to in my work and personal experience.

Although this book is written incorporating the woman-marrying-man paradigm (mostly to make the writing process simpler for simple me), the concepts outlined here apply to all couples regardless of sexual orientation or identification. These issues are not gender specific by any stretch so men should feel comfortable diving in, too.

On a personal note, I'm remarrying at this writing because I can feel good about my answers to the hard questions presented in this book. I want to same clarity for you, too. Whether you're marrying for the first time or the fourth, the time to determine whether this man is the best choice for you is now.

Getting engaged isn't an endpoint; it's the beginning of the lifelong work in progress called marriage. Most folks are at their best in the glow of romantic love. I'm asking you to take a half-step back from the stupor and splash some cold water on your face. Then, have a seat and start reading.

I'm giving you gold here, ladies. It's yours for the taking.

CHAPTER ONE

Is It Love?

A wise mentor of mine describes marriage as a relationship in which you do and share things you don't do and share in any other relationship in your life. At least ideally. This includes being in love in a way so powerful and unique that you want to partner with your loved one for life.

So, let's start there. Hopefully, this won't be a tough one. Does the love you have for this man trump any other you've had? If you're scratching your head, can you say it at least comes close? Are you able to think of another lover, partner, mate (you choose the label) who was a better love match for you? Do you ever pine for the kind of love you shared with that person?

I'm not talking about the hot, Swedish ski instructor and that après-ski quickie in the sauna. I'm not talking about great sex, puppy love or prom dates. I'm talking about love, love, love, love, crazy love. I'm talking about the kind of love that turns your world on end. The kind of love that makes your knees weak and your heart strong. If you've had it, you know it.

You may not remember the color of his eyes or his brother's name or the type of car he drove but you do remember how you *felt*. The way your heart raced when he asked for your number. The way he looked at you when you talked. The way you would

1

look for him across a room and find he was already staring. The way you both believed you had found your soulmate. All that and mind-blowing sex, too. Yep, you know the guy. You. Know.

And then it ended. And it was sad - so sad that your sister had to come up from Rhode Island to stay and you cried so much you eschewed wearing mascara for months just in case. Maybe you stayed single for a long while after or maybe you jumped into a rebound relationship. Hopefully, after the dust of your heartbreak settled, you were able to be grateful for the experience of having had such a great love.

Luckily, this type of love relationship is not limited to one per person. Many folks have several in a lifetime. Be it your tenth time at the rodeo or your first, you're now all out, full-throttle, balls to the wall (that's a piloting term, dirty girl) in love.

Wait. I'm sorry. Aren't you?

You are marrying a man who makes you euphoric with love, right? You do feel those butterflies when he reaches for your hand, correct? Look, for most people, this kind of *lurve* doesn't last beyond a couple of years. That's to be expected. But if you don't have it at the start of your relationship, you're never going to have it. You're not going to wake up one morning, see your husband's dirty socks on the floor and suddenly feel flush with new love. Not happening. And if it's not happening now, it's never going to happen to you again. Ever. In your life. *Capisce?* Because this is it. Your one shot at your last shot at gooey, yummy, dizzy, sticky love.

"Well," you may be saying to yourself, "gooey and dizzy are not important to me. Gooey and dizzy don't last. And there are other things much more important to me." To which I say, okay. You know you and what you need.

But, I might query, what about that other guy? Those things were important to you when you were with *him*, weren't they? There was a reason you stayed in that relationship as long as you did, right? You wanted gooey and sticky and you got it. And, don't be fooled, the desire - the need- for gooey love does not go away after you marry and it certainly does not go away as you age.

Wanting to be swept off your feet is okay at any stage in life. Wanting your heart to skip a beat when you kiss your man is also more than okay. If it's important to you, it's important to you. Don't write it off. Tell your partner you need passionate love. If you already have it in spades, express your appreciation for it. Let your man know that this aspect of your relationship is supremely important to you. Do your part to keep the embers burning. Don't try to convince yourself that it won't matter in the future because it will. Don't belittle your desire for crazy love as immature or inconsequential. It's neither.

Maybe you've had the experience before or you now want it for the first time. Perhaps you can acknowledge it's missing in your current relationship and you're longing for it. If that's the case, hats off to you. That means there's still time to do something about it. If it's lacking, you and your fiancé can work to make improvements in this area. Finding time for romance may give you enough of the crazy love you need to make it good enough. And only you can define what is good enough for you.

My guess is there are some of you who aren't feeling crazy love for your guy. Maybe you've never felt it for anyone. Maybe it's in your DNA or karma or astrological sign that this kind of love is not in the cards for you. To be clear, that's okay. Don't go running from what you have to find something that isn't that important to you. Wanting crazy love and *ignoring* that need is the issue. Not having it and being fine with that is just fine, too.

If you want and have it, remember that it may not be gooey and dizzy for all the days of your lives. But couples who can access gooey from time to time and can remember what it felt like when they had it, have a far greater chance of success than those who can't.

There's a well-established therapist's parlor trick I sometimes employ with the couples I work with. Basically, I ask the couple to describe the beginnings of their relationship. I listen to each person describe what it was like when they met, what they felt at that time, what the prevailing emotions were for them. I ask them to be as detailed as possible. What did they first notice about each other? When did they first realize they were in love? Sometimes this is a tough exercise because, let's face it, couples aren't usually in therapy to talk about how great their relationships are.

Almost immediately, it's apparent what the quality of the emotional relationship was like at its origins. Couples who were initially happy and loving can't help telling their story with sweet emotion. Even in the midst of their current strife, they can share a smile or loving giggle when reminiscing about their first days and months together. Conversely, couples who were initially stressed or unhappy have a harder time conjuring up any warmth or remembering loving moments. Their current disappointment and anger can so often be traced to the beginnings of their relationship.

Studies have shown that couples who can access warm, tender memories from the origins of their relationship have a better chance of success simply because all that wonderful feeling is part of their foundation.

Think about it.

CHAPTER TWO

How's the Sex?

W hat makes each of us sexually attracted to one person and not another is one of life's greatest and most delicious conundrums. Numerous studies have been conducted on physiology and pheromones and their influence on how we choose our sexual partners. But we don't need research to tell us why we're sexually attracted to someone. We just know that *we are*.

So, are you?

Frequency of sex can't predict success in marriage. Quality is totally subjective. Good sex at the beginning of a relationship isn't necessarily a great predictor of a marriage's longevity either. Lovingly tended, though, a sexual relationship that satisfies both partners can be an asset in any long-term relationship. Bad sex (and I don't mean naughty-bad) is a different story.

If you're wondering just what bad sex is because you just don't understand the concept, good for you! If you're wondering what bad sex is because you're not sure, you may want to pay close attention here.

Bad sex can be marked by any of the following:

- Frequency of sex that is uncomfortably high or low
- Experimentation (sexual positions or acts) that feels inherently uncomfortable
- Lack of attraction to or desire for your partner
- Anorgasmia (inability to have an orgasm, especially if you're able to have one yourself or have had them with other partners)
- Discomfort with telling your man what you like or don't like in bed
- A partner's insensitivity to your sexual needs or enjoyment level during sex
- Not feeling sexually aroused and just enduring it

To clarify, this list is for couples who have healthy, intact sexual histories and identities. If any of the above items are present in your relationship due to sexual trauma, abuse, or confusion about sexual orientation, that's another story altogether. If that's the case, I urge you to seek help with your partner so that you can respectfully co-create a sexual relationship that honors your (or your partner's) experience.

Now then.

If you'd rather do almost anything else with your man except have sex, then, Houston, we have a problem. Do men and women with very low libidos find each other and live happily ever after without having a lot of sex? Of course. But most of us aren't in that category. Most of us agree that sex is important in life and in marriage.

Because sexual quality and fulfillment are completely subjective, only you know whether you find your sex life satisfying. Hopefully, if you see your relationship somewhere on the bad sex list, you can bring your concerns to your partner.

Some of the items on the list can be addressed in a loving relationship. If you feel like you'd rather die than tell your man that you need oral-sex-every-time-no-byes, that's an issue. Sex is about communication and you need to find a way to get your point across. If you can't say it, write it. If you can't write it, find an article about it and forward it to him. Do whatever it takes to make the sex work for you.

Randall and Stacey sought my help as their 20-year marriage was crumbling. Stacey had just discovered that Randall had been having an affair for two years. She was stunned to learn Randall had never been happy with their sex life despite the fact that they had three children and fairly regular sexual relations. With enormous difficulty, Randall confessed that he had tired of always being the one to approach Stacey for sex and of her seeming lack of enjoyment when she did acquiesce. Even though Randall loved Stacey, he admitted he had gone outside the marriage for satisfying sex for many years. Now their marriage was ending in heartbreak.

In Randall and Stacey's scenario, it was he who was dissatisfied with their sex life. This is also *molto importante*, ladies. Does your fiancé seem satisfied with your current sex life? Does he want you to wear lingerie but wearing it makes you feel self-conscious? Is receiving oral sex from you important to him but it's not something you've ever enjoyed? Check in with yourself and let your gut tell you where you stand on his requests. If they're okay with you, go for it. You may just find that pleasing him heightens your enjoyment, too. If they just don't feel right and you're pretty sure they never will, tell him no. Then it's up to him to decide if he can forge a satisfying sex life with you without crotchless panties or blow jobs.

Because, and here's a newsflash if you haven't already tuned in, people *will* find a way to have their sexual needs met. Sex is funny that way. It's a drive that few are willing to ignore. If your husband doesn't satisfy you in bed, you *will* find a way to get your needs met. There are, of course, a variety of ways to make that happen but one strong possibility is that you will go outside the marriage. Shocking, right? Not really. Therapists' offices are backlogged with couples trying to work through affairs. It's positively pandemic.

When I trained in affair work, the commonplace belief was that an affair was just a symptom of a globally unhappy marriage. The thinking was that people went outside of their marriages for the connection and intimacy presumably lacking inside their marriages. That is true in many cases but not all. Recent research shows that some folks have affairs just to get their physical needs met. It appears you don't have to feel like your spouse doesn't understand you to go cry on someone else's libido. Maybe your spouse does understand you and is a good friend. But maybe he just can't give you what you need in bed and you're willing to risk a lot to get it.

I've offended you? My apologies. But while you're murmuring, "I would *never...*" under your breath, remember that some statistics show that nearly 50 percent of married women have affairs. The numbers are even higher for men. If you have taken offense, ask yourself why. Do you have concerns that your sex life is lacking but have already made a solemn promise to yourself that you'll just live with it the way it is? Just asking.

Remember: This is the last man you're ever going to have sex with. Ever. Read that again, please. And if you think it's okay that your sex life isn't good, think again. Are you willing to go the rest of your life not getting your sexual needs met or having sex with a man who bores or even repels you in bed?

Lucy, a 44-year-old client, is a talented photographer and avid cyclist. She knew when she married Davis fifteen years ago that their sex life was, "just not good."

Lucy says, "Even before we got married, I used to just lie there with my eyes closed waiting for the sex to be over. I would go somewhere else in my head and almost pretend I wasn't there. I married Davis because he had everything else. He was really successful and handsome. We shared the same deep religious beliefs. I just felt like, well, no one gets everything and good sex is the thing I wasn't going to get."

Prior to meeting Davis, Lucy had been in a relationship that brimmed over with sexual passion. She left that relationship to be with Davis, a decision she regrets. Lucy now has a lover and is considering divorce. There are, of course, other factors involved in the deterioration of their marriage but Lucy cites the bad sex as having a huge impact on her long-term unhappiness.

Like the experience of crazy love, sexual desire and passion normally don't increase with the longevity of a relationship. If you're one of the lucky ones (read: your marriage has a good sexual foundation and you both work hard at keeping that alive), you'll find that the intimacy you experience during sex will increase even when the wild passion decreases. Yes, you will always be able to find that one couple who claims their sexual desire for each has never waned – or has increased over time! But, sorry to say, sister, that probably won't be you. Especially if your relationship isn't strong sexually to begin with.

A 50-year-old friend of mine, Lisa, recalled this prophetic story from her twenties: "I was out one night with my friend, Marion, who had this amazing boyfriend named Johnny. Everyone loved this guy. He was smart, ambitious, and gorgeous. He treated her like a queen. Frankly, we were all a bit jealous of their relationship. She told me Johnny had started talking with her about getting married. She was hesitant. I remember saying to her, 'Are you nuts? He's terrific!' Her response to me was, yes, he was wonderful, but she just wasn't that attracted to him and the sex wasn't great. Instantly, I thought, 'That's exactly how I feel about Joe,' who I was planning to marry later that same year. I went ahead and married Joe. She didn't marry Johnny. She found someone better for her. I was divorced fifteen years later."

Like my client Lucy, Lisa admits there were a myriad of factors that contributed to her divorce but she remembers that conversation with her friend as a warning sign she ignored.

If I'm being totally honest," Lisa says, "I didn't even enjoy kissing him. I thought the other positive qualities in our relationship would smooth that over. I was wrong. Ten years into the marriage, I had an affair. Shortly after that, I left. I often reflect on that conversation with Marion and am always astonished by how willing I was to disregard it."

Lisa ignored the gift of Marion's story. So, I'm re-gifting her story here for you. Please feel free to keep it or re-gift it to anyone you feel could use it.

You'll thank yourself later.

CHAPTER THREE

Are You Loved As Is?

P art of the deliciousness of falling in love is having another recognize how pretty terrific you really are. You always suspected your greatness was in there somewhere and now it's been confirmed. Or maybe your fiancé has had to work hard to convince you of your amazingness. Either way, this man has chosen to be with you because of all the things that make you so uniquely attractive. You have finally found the one other who gets you in all your complexity and loves you because of it and, sometimes, in spite of it.

Sharing the same values, religion, or culture can make falling in love that much easier. Birds of a feather and all that. We flock to people similar to us. It just makes communication that much simpler. We understand each other. That also feels good. But what happens if you and your betrothed encounter fundamental differences that can make or break your relationship?

When I met my first husband over 25 years ago, he was a practicing Jew. Practicing, actually, doesn't cover it. He had practiced and perfected the art of living as an observant Jew. He kept a kosher kitchen, didn't shop or do laundry on Saturdays and celebrated several of the minor Jewish holidays many Jews haven't even heard of. He never visited his observant grandparents without donning a *yarmulke*. Friday nights were devoted to *Shabbat* dinner complete with lighting candles and saying the blessings over the bread and wine.

To this day, there's a lot of beauty and ritual to these practices that attract me. Then, I felt as if I'd been asked to relocate to the moon and open a 7-Eleven there. That's how foreign it all felt to me despite the fact that I have a Jewish father and grew up celebrating Passover and Hannukah with my Jewish grandparents.

Almost immediately, I realized that if I was going to be with this man, I would have to adopt his lifestyle. His way of life was ingrained in him. There was no compromising. As our relationship progressed and talk of spending our lives together began, the stakes got higher. Because my mother is not Jewish, strict Jewish law decreed that I would have to undergo an Orthodox conversion to Judaism to comply with the standards my boyfriend adhered to.

There are at least a dozen reasons I thought this seemed like a fine idea at the time. Chiefly, I had always been envious of folks who had religion in their lives. (My parents rejected it.) I also admired his intact extended family (my own family was deeply fractured) and saw their religious practice as something that had facilitated that.

I didn't realize it, but I was committing the serious relationship faux pas of looking to someone else to fill in my blanks, a topic more fully addressed later in this book. To clarify: There is nothing inherently wrong with changing your life. Sometimes it's the best thing you can do for yourself. However, changing your lifestyle and/or your belief system to comply with someone else's standards is another can of worms. Especially if you have little say in what that change is going to look like. No matter how big the red bow on top of the box, when you commit to a permanent lifestyle change in a relationship, you need to get clear about what the contents of the package will mean for you.

Some of you will wander into changes in your lifestyles you had no way of anticipating. Everyday women who marry celebrities can't possibility understand what that life will look like until they're in it. Marrying and living with someone with a physical handicap or chronic illness will also present unforeseen challenges. Becoming a military spouse requires sacrifice for country at a whole new level. The list goes on. What's important, as always, is how those challenges and changes are managed so that both partners have a voice and a vote.

I went ahead with the conversion. It was a lengthy and difficult process and, in many ways, both humiliating and inspiring. Regardless, I knew if I didn't go through with it, my boyfriend wouldn't marry me. Simple as that.

No one held a gun to my head. I made the decision to convert freely and willingly. I thought it would bring a depth to my life that was lacking. In many ways it did, but the cost was high. Among other sacrifices, I agreed to eschew my family's (non-religious) Christmas celebration which had always meant a great deal to me. My soon-to-be husband was just not comfortable with it. It also meant that my children would never have Christmas with my family. This deeply hurt my mother, especially, and for that I am forever ashamed.

What does it mean if your man is requesting that you change your life in a profound way or he will not marry you? Non-negotiable demands, as a rule, aren't healthy in any relationship. Part of the problem is that many of us are willing to twist ourselves into pretzels to fit the ideal our man wants. This is especially true at the beginning of a relationship when we're so in love we can't see straight. You want to please him so you're vulnerable to making choices that may not seem so dreamy and romantic a few years down the road.

Many of us will make changes in order to make a life with the man we love. That's okay. It's the quality of those changes that need to be held up to the light. Does he disapprove of your job and demand you rethink your career choice? Does he expect you to stay home with the kids full-time even though that's not your preference? Is there a paradigm being created in which his values and traditions clearly take precedence over yours?

Gretchen, a lovely 45-year-old client of mine, describes the beginnings of her marriage:

"Lance came from a very prominent, very wealthy family. Mega-wealthy. Although I grew up in relative comfort, I had never known anything like this: private jets and box seats everywhere we went. It was crazy and exciting and a little scary. My future in-laws couldn't have been kinder and I truly loved Lance."

"It became clear early on," Gretchen continues, "that the lifestyle his parents afforded us didn't come for free. We were expected to show up on every holiday regardless of what my family had planned. I didn't understand my mother's issues with it all then. I didn't get that being invited to some zillionaire's Christmas extravaganza wasn't the same as hosting her own holiday with her family."

Gretchen continues, "There was also the expectation that we would live very close to my in-laws and always vacation with them. They had much more access to my kids when they were growing up than my own parents did. And, of course, as the kids got older, the lifestyle was very cool and exciting to them as well. Although they love my parents, nothing can compare to the luxury and excitement my in-laws can offer. My parents are wonderful people and I know I've hurt them over the years and dashed their dreams of being a bigger part of my life and my kids' lives.

"I also never self-actualized," Gretchen admits with a wry smile. "I married very young and gave up my own dreams to fit the image expected by Lance and his parents. It all sounds very glamorous, I know, but it's a pretty empty existence."

Now, dear reader, I forgive you if you're thinking, "Yeah, well, poor baby having to fly around on private planes and never worrying for one moment about finances." Fair enough. But remember what we said regarding getting clear about the contents of the box attached to the red bow? Gretchen was presented with the red bow to end all red bows. Hers was so shiny and big, she couldn't resist it. Sadly, the expectations in the box required she make sacrifices that would eventually fill her with sadness and regret.

That's why the nature of change *for* a relationship needs to be carefully scrutinized. Any change comes with its challenges and difficulties. Just its definition indicates that we are taking on something new or different. Getting married is a huge lifestyle change that comes with its own adjustments and growing pains. Piling on mandatory prerequisites stipulated by your fiancé will likely lead to disappointment, self-doubt, and resentment.

Years ago, I read an advice column in a men's magazine. A reader had written seeking advice on whether he should marry his sweetheart. She was the perfect woman for him, he claimed, and he couldn't imagine his life without her. There was a rub, however. The love of his life was flat-chested and he didn't think he could marry her unless she agreed to have breast implants.

Huh?

Of course, the columnist wrote back with thoughtful advice on how that shouldn't matter, blah, blah, blah. If he was convinced she was his soul mate, the columnist responded, then, of course, he should marry her regardless of her cup size!

Imagine, for a moment, the plight of his poor girlfriend. Her man claims his undying love for her but only if she agrees to increase the size of her ta-tas? I don't know about you but I, for one, hope she ran for her life.

And this goes both ways, sweetheart. Ask yourself whether you are making do-or-die demands of your fiancé. I always ask my betrothed clients the same questions and now I am asking them of you: Are you happy with this person *as he is*? Do you find yourself thinking about ways he could change that would better suit you? If this man were never to change his looks, job, education or ambitions, would that be okay with you?

Getting married with an eye toward changing someone is a recipe for disaster. Is it okay to try to get him to wear cool jeans rather than the ones from JC Penney he's had since high school? Sure. Is it okay to get your cheeseburger-and-fries guy to branch out gastronomically? Of course. Those things are fine as long as *he* is fine with them. The bottom line is your fiancé is who he is and that needs to be more than fine with you.

I've seen many women treat their fiancés like real-life Ken dolls. These ladies want to dress their men up, polish their manners, and raise their tax brackets. In short, they want to create a man more in line with their ideal.

Treating your partner like a work-in-progress is not the way to start a marriage. You've agreed to marry this man because, ostensibly, you want to marry *this* man. If you want an updated, improved version of your man, find one. And if he's asking you to be a Barbie doll and you're really a Flatsy, be clear about what it would mean for you to honor his request. Then, if your gut tells you no-go, point him in the direction of the nearest toy store.

CHAPTER FOUR

Want Kids?

You may want to skip this chapter if you and your betrothed have already made that iron-clad, never-in-a-million-years decision not to have children. What's that, you say? You're pretty sure it's iron clad? You're almost positive you don't want kids?

Keep reading.

A hundred years ago (okay, it only feels that way) when I was pregnant with my second child, I met another pregnant mom at a parenting class. I already had a son and, of course, assumed I'd have a daughter on the second go-round. Isn't that the way it's supposed to happen? Son First + Daughter Second = Perfectly Balanced Family?

In any case, I shared with her how completely different this pregnancy was from my first and, because of that, I was absolutely certain this baby was going to be a girl (see family math equation above).

"Well, even if I don't have a boy this time around," she replied, (she had a firstborn daughter), "I'm all set. My husband and I have an agreement. We keep going until we have one child of each gender." (Footnote: I had another boy).

I remember being stunned by her response. Just the fact that she and her husband had such a mature and thoughtful contract around this issue threw me. Why didn't I think of that? Why don't most people?

Many couples have the how-many-kids conversation. That's a good place to start and I hope you and your fiancé have already had it. But it may not be enough. My whole life I wanted four children and I told my ex-husband that before we married. Later, he insisted I had said I only wanted two children. Not so. It was he who initially wanted two children (we had three) and somehow heard that I agreed with him. Needless to say, this misunderstanding created a great deal of stress in the marriage.

This is not a one-off conversation to be had with your fiancé after three margaritas. If you have shared religious views that pre-determine you will welcome any number of children, go forth and multiply! Despite our religious beliefs, however, most of us need to consider other factors, including finances and personal visions for our own lives outside of parenting responsibilities. This can be complex, *chicas*.

Many years ago, I had a 37-year-old client, Juliet, who had married a successful entrepreneur in his late fifties. Mark had made it clear from the get-go that having kids was not an option. He had *beentheredonethat* and had two grown kids from his first marriage. It was not something he was willing to do again.

At the outset, Juliet was in full agreement. She had a busy, productive life and a demanding career in the travel industry. Her work necessitated that she travel several weeks out of the year. Having children had never been high on her life to-do list.

She'd had other offers of marriage and, partially because she wasn't focused on her biological clock, she had refused them. When Mark came along, Juliet was thrilled. The kid question, it seemed, was asked and answered by both of them. They had so much in common and looked forward to a fun and comfortable life together.

But then.

Juliet started to have stirrings. Most of her siblings and friends had or were having children and she started to take notice. The ticking of her biological clock got louder and louder. The stirrings got stronger and eventually morphed into an undeniable yearning. She wanted kids! Who knew?

Juliet approached Mark with her newfound desire. She wanted to be a mom. Many discussions and heated arguments ensued. Mark felt duped and cornered. He had made it clear at the start of the relationship that having kids would not be part of his second marriage. After many months of tears and recriminations, Mark caved. He loved Juliet and wanted her to be happy. Despite his many reservations, Mark did not want to be the one to deprive Juliet of the experience of being a mom.

Juliet got pregnant easily. She was thrilled and Mark even seemed quietly pleased. Not long into the pregnancy, they discovered Juliet was pregnant with twin boys. This discovery set them back. Not only had Mark not wanted one child, now he was getting two. Mark's anger and resentment resurfaced often culminating in emotional discussions with Juliet that lasted long into many nights. Juliet was angry as well. How could Mark be upset by this blessing? Who was this guy she married, anyway?

When the boys were born, one was quickly diagnosed with Down's syndrome. For some reason, this had not been detected in any of Juliet's prenatal testing. Both Juliet and Mark were blindsided. This was something neither of them had signed on for. Mark, especially, was emotionally flattened by the news. He had a nephew with Down's and knew raising this son was going to entail challenges he had never anticipated. Closing in on 60, Mark was already exhausted by the thought.

A year after bringing the boys home, Juliet and Mark separated. Although Mark loved his sons, living with them proved too much for him. He was perpetually angry with Juliet for creating a situation he never wanted to begin with. Their marriage became an unhealthy mix of resentment and rage and both agreed it would be better for the boys if they lived apart.

Juliet and Mark's story is a good example of how couples can get lost on this issue. As discussed in the last chapter, you need to accept that your fiancé is representing who he is and who he will remain. If he is saying he won't consider having more than one child, you must assume that will be the case. You must not go into marriage thinking, "Well, once he sees how adorable our firstborn is, he'll definitely want more." Usually doesn't work that way.

Unlike painting your house green or white, driving a coupe or a minivan, or living in the city or the 'burbs, having a baby is not a decision you can be wishy-washy about. You can't compromise and have half a baby and you can't blow this decision off as something TBD later on.

Expect to negotiate. Most couples do on this issue. Hear him out and make sure he hears you. If he wants a small family and you've always wanted a chaotic houseful, are you willing to make that sacrifice? Is your decision being made happily and willingly?

Come to an agreement. Write it down and sign it if you like. A contract may come in handy when one of you wavers from your initial understanding. This doesn't mean that as time goes on you can't renegotiate. Life throws us curveballs and sometimes the reality of having twelve kids just isn't in the cards or the bank account. Attempting to emotionally strong-arm your spouse into having more or fewer children is never going anyplace good. Know that.

Couples should also come up with agreements regarding infertility treatment, adoption, abortion and other unexpected circumstances. What is your agreement if you discover you are carrying a severely disabled child? Would you both be okay using a surrogate if you're unable to carry a child yourself? A husband of one client of mine has a very low sperm count and is unable to impregnate his wife. He refuses to use donor sperm despite the fact that my client desperately wants to bear a child. Where would your man stand on this? Where would you?

Start by asking questions and having conversations. As with divorce, many of us would like to think these situations won't apply to us. You may expect that you will get pregnant easily and carry healthy babies to term. I hope that will be true. But it's not always that simple. For many couples, the road to building a family is a bumpy one so try your best to pave the way now.

CHAPTER FIVE

Tell Me Where It Hurts

Your partner has the unique ability to tap into your deepest emotional wounds and activate them in a way no other can. Think about it. Who else can make you as angry? Who else can hurt you as deeply and profoundly? No one? Exactly. You have the ability to, "cut each other's hearts out with a spoon," a phrase my guy often so eloquently borrows. This is what I have termed Wound Tapping.

In romantic relationships, one way you make yourself highly vulnerable to your partner is by sharing your more difficult formative experiences. He knows about the babysitter who was inappropriate with you. About the high school boyfriend who broke your heart. He knows about the college date rape. And that your mother had an affair with your seventh grade math teacher. He knows that you carry those ten extra pounds because food was scarce in your house growing up and now eating is complex for you. Some of your wounds were seeded in childhood and those usually run the deepest.

Look, if your childhood was perfect, your parents were perfect, your siblings were perfect, your clergy and neighbors were perfect, your friends and teachers and coaches were perfect then, by all means, declare yourself wound-free and stop reading here.

Oh, you're still here?

Of course you are. Every one of us has emotional wounds and sore places that we have carried with us from childhood into adulthood.

The vulnerability in love relationships mimics the openness you had as a child. Defenseless against parents and caretakers, children are vessels, wide open to whatever is poured into them. If you've been fortunate, most of your care was good or even good enough. Even in the best of circumstances, however, children are wounded by the very same people who love and care for them. Why? Because these people, usually your parents, are also wounded by their own experiences. It's an infinity cycle: they're hurt, they hurt you, you're wounded and, yes, you'll eventually wound your own kids. And so it goes.

Ironically, Wound Tapping (WT) can be the biggest gift and the strongest glue for many couples and I'll get to that in a minute. But here's the strangest thing about WT: we always, but *always*, find ourselves with partners who will unwittingly (at least at first) activate those hurt places in us. Sounds crazy, right?

Married only a year, my client Alice discovered her husband was being unfaithful when she found another woman's earring on the floor of his truck. When confronted, Carlo admitted he had never stopped seeing other women during the course of their relationship. He was, in fact, a sex addict. Carlo's childhood story was ghastly. His father had sexually abused him and had encouraged two of his uncles to do so as well. His mother did little or nothing to stop any of it. There was also ample physical abuse in their home.

We don't need to channel Sigmund Freud to understand where Carlo's unhealthy sexual addiction stemmed from. His warped sense of what was appropriate in sexual matters was skewed by the gross inappropriateness of the adults around him. Carlo was attracted to sweet Alice partly because she came from a relatively intact family that certainly seemed safer to him than his own family of origin.

But what drew Alice to Carlo? Alice's family dynamic was indeed somewhat healthier than Carlo's and she felt good about being the more stable force in their relationship. Alice had, however, grown up with an alcoholic father and bipolar mother. Her mother was a difficult woman who spent most of her marriage accusing her husband of infidelity, which he vehemently denied.

Alice never believed her father was unfaithful despite the fact that her mother seemed to have proof. Still, her father's addiction to alcohol and his alleged betrayals occupied Alice's most vulnerable core. Carlo's behavior, therefore, tapped into Alice's deepest wounds. He was the embodiment of the two behaviors she feared the most in marriage: addiction and infidelity.

Many of us "hire on" our potential spouses to activate or reactivate our childhood wounds. Everything we know about relationships we learned in childhood and that knowledge becomes like a pair of well-worn slippers. We keep wearing them even when they're not all that comfortable anymore.

Why, you might ask, would I look for someone who is going to create pain for me? Why would I marry someone who hurts me and makes me feel like crap? Good questions. The answers are complex but you can take solace in the fact that so many of us do it unwittingly. The good news is that WT is not a relationship death sentence. In fact, knowing your spouse's wounded places can be a wonderful thing. We're getting to that. Hang on.

Ideally, you should know your own wounded places as well

as your fiancé's. This can and will take some work. It may also take some time for your wounded places to reveal themselves in the context of your relationship. For those of you who come from good enough families of origin, they may be buried deeper. But make no mistake, they are there.

Let's take a closer look at Alice. She knew she never, ever wanted to marry an alcoholic. She saw what her dad's alcoholism did to her family and the havoc it wreaked. When she met Carlo, she was relieved to discover that he didn't drink. Eureka, right? Wrong. Instead, she married someone with another type of addiction which ended up causing her just as much pain as if he had been a raging alcoholic. She unintentionally replaced one addiction with another.

Ideally, Carlo would have been aware of Alice's wounded places and Alice would have been more able to talk about them. If she had been able to express that addiction and infidelity were her greatest fears, perhaps she and Carlo would have been able to build a marriage that respected and healed those hurts rather than triggered them. Not surprisingly, Alice and Carlo divorced.

So how, pray tell, do you unscramble this romantic DaVinci Code? For one thing, you and your fiancé should make it a point to talk about your families of origin. Think about your parents' marriage. What were the dynamics? In the absence of any florid behaviors (addictions, abuse, affairs), what can you identify as issues in their relationship? What was the power dynamic in their marriage? Did each have a voice and was it heard? What do you and your fiancé argue about? Is the topic usually the same or similar?

My own parents' marriage was fraught with accusations of infidelity and its best buddy, romantic jealousy. In almost every relationship I've had, I've brought these two bugaboos with me.

My parents had many other issues in their marriage but this one left me with deeply complex wounds.

My fiancé grew up as the oldest son of three kids. His mother was very loving and he adores her to this day. His dad, a successful physician, provided well for his family but had an explosive temper of which my fiancé was often the target. When his father did get angry at him, he would often go days without speaking to him. As you might imagine, this created an enormous amount of stress and anxiety for my fiancé as a young man.

Although my guy has had several long-term, committed relationships during his adult life, he never let go an opportunity to get an eyeful of any attractive woman to cross his path. I experienced this blatant, lustful staring as rude and disrespectful. Apparently, I was the first woman in his life to tell him to Cut. This. Shit. Out. His behaviors obviously triggered my adorable twin wounds: Jealousy and Insecurity.

Because these wounds went so deep for me, so went my anger. I would become explosively angry and enormous arguments would ensue. See where this is headed? As a child, he experienced his father's anger as the potential loss of love and safety. My anger would trigger those same fears in him. When I get angry, he fears he will lose me or, at the very least, I will punish him emotionally.

After some couples counseling and a lot of soul-searching, we are now able to recognize these wounds in the other and treat them with care. He has worked very hard to change the behaviors that are so wounding for me and I have worked very hard to curb my anger. Is it now perfect? No. But we're both aware of the impact we have on the other and we work very hard to be gentle with each other's wounds.

The ultimate goal is to recognize each other's wounds and help heal them. This is where WT can be a wonderful experience that strengthens and deepens your relationship. Perhaps your fiancé's mother was withholding with her praise. Despite the fact that he tried hard to earn her accolades, he never got the feeling that she was proud of him. This left him with the wound of not feeling good enough or worthy of admiration. See where you come in?

Yep, by showering your man with loving praise and appreciation for his efforts, you are giving him what was so lacking in his experience with his mother. You are providing him with the chance to heal from something that left a big hole in his development and psyche. Conversely, if you tap into this wound in an unhealthy way, you may find yourself constantly criticizing him or expressing disappointment in his efforts. This mimics his mother's behavior and keeps that wound open for him.

Wound Tapping is a very complex, unconscious process. The examples in this chapter are designed to help you begin thinking about how WT is present in your relationship. Once you begin to ferret out how you and your fiancé engage in WT together, you'll deepen your relationship in a way that will allow for greater empathy and less fighting. And don't we all want that?

CHAPTER SIX

Fill in Your Own Blanks

You are signing up for a boatload of disappointment and regret if you're expecting either your man, or marriage itself, to whisk you away to a ready-made and fulfilling life. This isn't a fairy tale, sister. Your man doesn't have magic powers that will fill in your gaps and make your life whole. And though you should feel like your partner makes you a better person, you're just an improved version of an already good enough one. With or without this man in your life, you should be who you want to be, living the satisfying life you want to live.

Hollywood sells women a lot of rescue fantasy crap. *Jerry Maguire*, for example, was at its core, a fun, entertaining Cinderella story. To recap: single, kinda cute, struggling mom, Dorothy (Renee Zellweger) falls for Jerry (Tom Cruise), a financially-stressed (but only briefly), ridiculously handsome, divorcing Alpha male with potentially outstanding fathering skills. Dorothy realizes that with some love, patience and support, Jerry will eventually find his way back to the top of the pile and beat his chest all the way to the bank.

Jerry's likely financial success (which, of course, Dorothy doesn't care about *at all* because, honestly, what woman has ever cared about *that?*) will remedy her money struggles and their relationship will provide her son with a loving Insta-Dad. She'll never have to go to college or learn to support herself. Her hardest challenge will have been raising her son alone for five years under the watchful eye of her bitchy sister.

Although kiddie lit has improved over time, most young girls' minds are flooded with traditional bedtime stories about young women rescued by men who will provide them with lives full of romance and untold riches. A prince's kiss brings her back to life, a handsome knight rescues her from imprisonment in a tower. We all know the drill and it's been drilled into us.

There is nothing inherently wrong with marrying someone who is going to improve your life in some form or fashion. It's likely (sad but true, ladies) that you will marry someone who makes more money than you, and that may make your life easier in some ways. Maybe this person has more schooling and that inspires you. Perhaps he loves to travel and shares the travel bug with you. All okay. Not okay if you're marrying someone who you believe can fundamentally complete *your* life with *his* ambitions and successes.

Earlier I described how my ex-husband's intact extended family and religious commitment attracted me. I was drawn to the abstract traits of a life that, at the time, I knew almost nothing about. In a matter of months, I had completely changed my lifestyle, food choices and relationship with my own family. The promise of the life I imagined I would have with him overshadowed any nagging doubts I allowed myself to feel. I plowed through the concerned questioning of family and friends. Nothing was going to stand in my way.

In retrospect, it was a house of cards. I was building a life on someone else's terms. I didn't go out and find religion for myself. I didn't ask myself what the psychological toll of living by someone else's rules would be. I didn't even look closely at the emotional culture and structure of his decidedly intact family.

I saw the white picket fence and I went for it. Of course, we all know that white picket fences are a boatload of work, need lots of paint and repair, and are often only pretty from the street.

Choose what you want your life to look like and live it now. Make sure you know what's important to you. Ask yourself what you're bringing to the marriage that you simply cannot compromise on. Fill in your own blanks and don't look to your partner to do that for you.

Answer this question: What does my fiancé bring to my life that I believe betters me? Make a list. Ideally it will look something like this:

1) A more hopeful way of looking at life
2) A commitment to recycling (or whatever) that has rubbed off on me in a good way
3) A better way of living that includes eating right and exercise
4) A healthy devotion to his family that I strive to emulate
5) A great work ethic that spurs me to work harder and more efficiently

It should not look like this:

1) A financial portfolio that wows me because of my own financial struggle
2) An education that impresses my family and friends and that I don't share
3) Connections to powerful people I would never have known without him
4) An address I never could have afforded
5) Interests that are the polar opposite of mine - but, that's okay, I'll get used to birdwatching in the Arctic in no time!

See the difference? The first list outlines ways your fiancé brings improvements to positive aspects in your life that are already in place. His commitment to these things raises the bar for you in a way that's healthy. It's all good.

At first glance, the second list isn't all bad. Nothing wrong with improving your financial lot or living in a nicer home. Certainly not. But where are *you* on List Two? If you're looking to ride your fiancé's coattails and impress others with his successes, you're signing up for your own long-term emptiness. His desires or ambitions may be lovely and lofty but, if they're not yours, then this marriage is going to have either a short, rocky shelf-life or a long, miserable one.

I have to believe that if you've gotten this far in the book, you're a thoughtful, intelligent woman asking yourself the right questions about your relationship. If you're starting to think you might be marrying someone who impresses your friends and family more than he lights your fire, I'm hoping this concerns you. Good-on-paper isn't worth the paper it's printed on. Know that.

Regardless, we're all a little bit guilty of wanting to be with the guy who is going to rescue us. Isn't that what you were taught to want, and what biology supports? An Alpha male who will provide for you and protect your family? And, biologically speaking, isn't your man looking for someone who he can impregnate easily and who will tend to his children while he's out fighting the good fight?

In my psychotherapy practice, I've worked with wives and ex-wives of professional athletes. The fame! The fortune! It's dizzying. Many of these women come from small towns and grew up in middle-class families. Then one day…*kapow!* They marry their high school or college sweethearts and find themselves in the Land of Whatever League Oz.

Carol, the ex-wife of a professional athlete who she met

while they were both in college, describes marriage to a professional athlete as an exercise in self-sacrifice.

"It's like being in the back of a pickup truck going down the bumpiest road you can imagine. Moving from city to city, uprooting your kids, and not knowing what the future will hold in terms of contracts or injuries. A lot of us wives get involved in charities but they're usually charities associated with the team. Your whole life is the team - supporting it, rooting for it, living for it. And even then there's no guarantee the marriage will last. And if it does end, you realize you've spent the last number of years chasing a dream that wasn't yours to begin with."

Carol's story is a cautionary tale. Divorced at 35, she awoke to the harsh reality that she had put her life on the back burner so she could support her husband's dreams that, she says, "somehow felt bigger and more important than mine."

Ladies, your dreams are yours and they are important! Find what moves you, wows you, and makes you jump out of bed in the morning. Is your career on the track that you'd like? Have you always dreamed of going to grad school? Is going to church every Sunday your goal? Then do one, do all! The list can be long and it should be. Your man should be on board and supportive of your list just as you should be of his.

Some items on your lists may overlap and others may create tensions that will necessitate compromise. No matter. What does matter is that you create a life that has meaning for you. Sometimes your man needs to be on the sidelines cheering you on and you will, of course, do the same for him. But if you're the one who's always waving the pom-poms, figure out a way to get on the field. And do it now.

CHAPTER SEVEN

Fighting and Forgiving

If you're with someone long enough, you're going to disagree. That's a given. If you insist that you and your fiancé never argue, disagree or see things differently, I don't know what to say. Congratulations? Buyer beware?

If you're among the other 99.9 percent of us, you know how difficult and painful it is to be in disagreement with your partner. Especially when you know you're right. Right? Kidding, ladies.

There's no magic spell that can prevent you and your man from arguing periodically throughout your lives together. Put any two people in the same house for more than a couple of weeks and you can pretty much sit back and watch the sparks fly. Reality TV has made that painfully clear.

So, it's not *that* you fight. It's *how* you fight.

I'm sure you're somewhat relationship savvy, dear reader, and know the basics about fighting with your man: stay on point, don't swear or insult, don't say anything you'll regret later, don't hurt each other physically (ever!) and, my personal favorite, don't threaten to leave unless you really mean it. That last one is a big ouch-y and opens the door, both figuratively and literally, to painful possibilities.

I don't know about you but I'm pretty sure I've done everything on that list except getting physical. Yes, even psychotherapists do what they advise their clients against. If you see your behaviors on that list, don't fret. It's not too late to make changes or to ask your man to do the same.

Fighting fairly and respectfully is essential to any healthy relationship. I'm assuming if you and your man have chosen to spend your lives together, you have a healthy respect for each other's points of view and feelings. That respect should not be thrown out the window when the fighting starts. In fact, when friction develops, respect should be your top priority.

Impossible, you say? Sometimes it feels that way. The goal, however, is to come out whole and healthy on the other side. The argument will eventually end so make a conscious decision that you will be okay with your behaviors during the argument once it's over.

Apologizing seems to come more naturally to women. Maybe it's in our nature to try and smooth things over. Perhaps we're just a little more willing to sacrifice pride in the name of keeping our relationships intact. Authentic apology is a beautiful, healing tool in any relationship. However, it's one you both need to employ. If you're the only one doing the I'm-sorry-let's-not-fight-I-was-wrong dance, then the balance is skewed. Remember, it takes two; you can't tango alone.

Your fiancé must be willing to apologize when he's in the wrong. When he apologizes to you, he's letting you know that he recognizes his behaviors were offensive and he's willing to own that. His apology confirms that he cares what you think and how his actions affect you. Saying he's sorry is saying he's more concerned about your hurt feelings than he is about his pride or being right.

Apologizing is money in the relationship bank. When you make healthy apology an organic part of your communication, it paves the way for it to happen more frequently and easily. Withholding apology does just the opposite. It establishes the dynamic "Why should I apologize? S/he never does!" And that's just plain crappy.

A healthy apology sounds something like this: "I'm really sorry I hurt you with my words and actions. I realize now that I behaved badly and wasn't being sensitive to your feelings. I hope you can forgive me. I'll do my best not to let it happen again." In this example, the apologizer is taking responsibility for his behavior, acknowledging how it affected you, is asking for forgiveness and is making a commitment to fix that behavior going forward.

An unhealthy apology sounds something like this: "I'm sorry you're upset/angry/embarrassed about what happened."

See the diff? In the unhealthy example, he's not only dismissing personal responsibility for his behaviors but is also putting the blame on you. He could easily be saying, "I'm sorry you're so sensitive and get pissed off so easily. It's unfortunate you're like that." That's not an apology, people. That's a blaming statement designed to make you feel like you're the one who behaved badly.

Accepting an apology graciously can also be challenging. When my sister and I were little and she would inadvertently (ahem) hurt me, she'd occasionally apologize. My response? "Well, it doesn't make the pain go away!"

That's how *not* to respond to an apology.

There is some truth, however, in my response to my sister. Although an apology can help soften the blow, it really doesn't make the initial injury go away. That's your challenge. Forgiving is not the same thing as forgetting so don't expect the two to go hand in hand. Keep in mind that you're forgiving a statement, action or behavior on the part of your fiancé. He's not repellent, his behavior was. If you have the ongoing feeling he's just a boorish ass, that's something else entirely. If his poor behaviors are ongoing despite his apologies, then it's time to take a second look. If he continues to hurt you in the same way and seems incapable of changing, you may want to seek some couples therapy in order to get to the bottom of what is going on for the two of you.

My clients, Polly and Jim, have been married for 25 years and have three children. Jim is a highly successful business consultant. Polly, a certified accountant, stopped working many years ago to stay home and raise their children. They came to see me when Polly found out Jim had secretly taken out a home equity loan without her consent.

Almost from the beginning of their marriage, Polly remembers that Jim seemed to lie easily. At first, there were small lies, like Jim saying he had paid a bill when he really hadn't. Over time, the lies got bigger. Money went missing from their bank accounts for which Jim always had a hazy excuse. He also took dubious business trips and kept secret credit cards and email accounts that Polly would eventually unearth.

Initially, Jim would apologize profusely for his behaviors. Jim would tell Polly he truly loved her and the kids and would do anything to keep their family together. Polly wanted the same. Among other things, Polly and Jim shared a strong sexual connection. They also could have a lot of fun sharing time with family and friends. As Polly said, "It wasn't all about Jim's lies. There were a lot of good things, too."

So, Polly would forgive. Then, she'd forgive again. Jim's behaviors persisted, however. Polly's forgiveness didn't spur Jim to change his behaviors, but only seemed to give him license to continue them.

Remember, ladies, when you forgive someone you are not only freeing yourself from your own pain and anger but you're also giving that person an invaluable gift. If your man can't appreciate and honor the gift of your forgiveness, he is negating what is at the core of every sustainable relationship: the ability to recognize the other as imperfect and to offer them the charity and love inherent in that recognition.

There are things that simply cannot be forgiven. Only you know where that line in the sand is for you. When faced with a breach, ask yourself whether forgiveness is a real possibility. Don't delude yourself that once you tie the knot it will be easier to forgive. Believe me, it won't matter less that your fiancé once slept with your maid of honor; it will matter more. It can quickly go from, "It bums me out that my boyfriend fooled around with my roomie," to "My husband was sexually intimate with my best friend!" The stakes feel much higher once you're married.

If there are things you question about your man's business dealings, his prior relationships, or his character, try to come to some resolution about them before you walk down the aisle. Ask yourself if these are things that will affect you or your relationship directly. Can you accept that he stole money from his roommate's wallet when he was in college? Can you excuse him for fudging his tax returns for the past five years? Are you still angry he dated your sister before he got around to asking you out? If he's been married before, does he treat his ex-wife respectfully?

None among us is perfect and all of us will cause our partners pain. Without honored and appreciated forgiveness, your relationship will wither. Without the willingness or ability to apologize, resentment will take root and grow.

Say you're sorry and expect him to do the same.

CHAPTER EIGHT

Adultery, Addiction and Abuse

Adultery

My clients, Naomi and Paul, are a lively, attractive couple in their early thirties. Shortly after their engagement, Naomi had a one-night stand with a male coworker. When Paul found out, he was devastated. Since confessing, Naomi has thrown herself into trying to repair the relationship. She has done everything she can think of to make Paul feel secure including working from a home office and giving Paul access to all of her files, emails and online activities.

Although Naomi has apologized many times for the affair, Paul is emotionally stuck. He can't forgive and he can't forget. He uses any and every disagreement they have to throw the incident in Naomi's face. If Naomi is late to an event (or any other negligible infraction), Paul wastes no time tying it to the infidelity. "This is just a reminder of how you marginalized me when you slept with that guy. It's all the same disrespectful behavior," is typical of something Paul would say.

There's no hard and fast rule that one must forgive an affair. It's certainly okay if Paul decides he isn't able to. In a healthy relationship, however, you can't have it both ways. You can't expect your partner to live an apologetic life while continuing to berate and blame him/her. Frankly, you can do whatever you want, but you need to ask yourself: What is it that you actually *want*? A satisfying, mutually respectful relationship? Or an unhappy home infused with insults, blame and tension?

For Naomi and Paul, her affair is an ongoing issue that likely will not be resolved in a satisfactory way. Both have serious and valid concerns about going through with their wedding. What would you do if you were Naomi or Paul?

If an affair is not a current issue in your relationship, have you and your partner discussed what would happen to your relationship if one of you had one? Okay, you might be thinking, who the heck talks about this stuff? Why stir the pot and make trouble where trouble doesn't exist?

Here's why: Couples like Naomi and Paul show up in therapists' office in droves every day. Affairs are rampant in our society. They're at epidemic numbers. Chances of a couple experiencing infidelity are reported at anywhere from 40 to 75 percent. Most of us hope the dark shadow of adultery won't cross our path. But what if it does?

Jackie, a close friend of mine, grew up in a home in which her father was a serial adulterer. Her mother irresponsibly shared her husband's extracurricular details with her children. Jackie suffered emotionally from the fallout from both her parents' inappropriate behaviors and knew she couldn't have those issues be part of her own marriage. Before she married Luke, she made it clear to him that she wouldn't tolerate infidelity. Jackie and Luke spent many hours discussing what would happen if one of them were to have an affair.

What they decided was to be especially sensitive to any feelings or behaviors in themselves or others that might lead to an affair. If any outside relationship started to feel more than platonic, they agreed to immediately tell each other and decide what to do about it. They even agreed to quit jobs or move if need be. They made a pact.

Jackie and Luke have now been married over twenty years. Although employing the rules of their agreement hasn't been necessary, they still revisit them from time to time. Says Jackie, "To some people, our pact may seem like overkill. The fact that we've promised to quit our jobs over a serious flirtation might seem crazy. But if you look around at what's going on in marriages today, it doesn't seem as out there. I'm grateful Luke was willing to commit to something that would help us and our kids avoid a lot of pain."

Be willing to raise this issue with your fiancé. If he saw his parents cheat or if he's been unfaithful in past relationships, explore these experiences with him and share your own. It's not always true, but past behaviors can be good indicators of future ones. Infidelity also seems to become part of a family's culture and legacy. Many people who experienced their parents being unfaithful are disappointed to find themselves repeating those behaviors.

On the topic of infidelity, no detail is too small to be addressed. It really isn't enough to say, "I'd be really hurt if you cheated on me." Talk about what kinds of behaviors are okay and which ones would make either or both of you uncomfortable. Is it okay with you if your partner looks at porn? How about if he befriends women at the office? Is his reconnecting with old girlfriends on Facebook comfortable for you? Is a one-night stand a forgivable infraction?

What about an ongoing affair? Do you want to know about it or would you rather employ a don't-tell policy? Are close, flirtatious relationships with others okay as long as they don't cross the line into the physical realm? Any and all arrangements are fine as long as they're fine with both of you. Remember, the rules need to apply unilaterally. There's no his-and-hers. What's good for the goose is, well, you know.

Map this out. Make your pact. And try like hell to stick to it.

Addiction

The beginning of a relationship should be a time of fun and frolic. You're falling in love, for Pete's sake! Everything he does just seems so dreamy and cool. So what that he cracks a beer at 10a.m.? He's on vacation! Does it really matter that he smokes pot every night "just to relax"? He works hard and deserves his down time! And, if they're being honest, don't most men look at online porn every day? He's just a really upfront and sexy guy!

For our purposes, I'm defining addiction as any habitual behavior or substance use that 1) Changes your man's mood state when he engages in it, and/or 2) Changes his mood state when he doesn't. What sets addiction apart from casual use is the *reliance* on the behavior or substance to create a feeling or mood that can't be evoked without it. Also, without the behavior or substance, his mood state plummets or changes dramatically.

I'm not setting out to malign your man's choices. Again, only you know what feels comfortable for you in your relationship. What is of concern is his control vis-à-vis these issues. Can he stop the drinking, drugging, porn use, gambling or [name-your-poison] whenever he wants without much difference in his personality or mood? Are these behaviors really just a form of casual entertainment or are they addictions that may turn out to play a big part in your life?

My client, Carla, 40, is an attractive and successful lawyer with two young daughters. She divorced her husband, Jason, after 15 unhappy years of marriage. Soon after, she met David, a hardworking entrepreneur. They fell madly in love. David, she thought, was everything that Jason wasn't. David was kind to her and made her feel good about herself. They also had an intense sexual connection - something she hadn't shared with Jason. Her marriage to Jason had lacked fun and spontaneity, but her relationship with David had those things in spades.

At the beginning of the relationship, Carla and David lived it up: travel, fine restaurants, and lots of socializing with friends. Alcohol was always part of their social life and both Carla and David enjoyed their cocktails. One night, while Carla was out of town, David met some friends for drinks. Returning home, he was pulled over and charged with driving under the influence. Shaken by David's experience, Carla began to rethink her lifestyle.

She began to notice that the time she spent with David always involved drinking. She also noticed she was drinking more than she ever had including pouring herself a glass of wine or two every night after work. Then she noticed that her daughters started noticing. The girls were young teens and Carla was worried she wasn't setting a good example.

Carla tried discussing her concerns with David. At first he agreed their lifestyle wasn't healthy. Carla and David agreed they would curb their drinking especially during the week when the girls were home.

Carla was happy with their agreement and felt that David understood and respected her concerns. Soon, though, Carla began to notice two things about David. One was that she could smell booze on David during the week despite their agreement. David had begun drinking secretly and lying about his whereabouts in order to do so. The other was that when David didn't drink in the evenings, he became surly and verbally aggressive toward Carla and would fly off the handle at the slightest provocation.

By the time Carla came to therapy, she was teary and at the end of her emotional rope. This man, who she had initially seen as an answer to her relationship prayers, was now becoming a nightmare to live with. When she approached him about their downward-spiraling relationship, David's comment was, "I haven't changed since we met, Carla. You're the one who is changing and asking me to change. I'm still the guy you fell in love with. I'm still the guy who enjoys his liquor."

And David had a point.

After many months, Carla made the tough decision to end their relationship. Their fighting and David's increasing secretiveness made staying in the relationship impossible. Heartbroken, Carla is now working through her pain and picking up the pieces of her life.

If you see yourself in Carla's story, take a closer look. What may feel like fun and games at the beginning of a relationship may not bode well for a lifetime. Take some time to closely scrutinize your man's habits and lifestyle choices. Are there behaviors you're concerned about or that others have worriedly pointed out to you?

One good way to analyze your concerns is to ask yourself these questions: Would I be embarrassed for others to know the extent of these behaviors? Is my current lifestyle one I would choose for my children?

You might be thinking, "I'm young. I want to have fun while I can!" or "My kids are grown now. I can finally do what I want!" Understood. But is your lifestyle with your man one that is positioned to bring you health and joy? Can you imagine a life in which these behaviors become problematic?

We all have ways to unwind and most things in moderation are fine. If you're concerned about any of these behaviors (or ones that aren't mentioned here), address them with your fiancé now. It will only get harder as time passes. Your silence is an indicator that his current behaviors are okay with you and that you're willing to live with them for the long run.

Physical Abuse

Physical abuse is never okay. Never. Okay. Okay?

Margo, 35, showed up in my office confused and agonizing about her marriage. She and Todd had been high school sweethearts and had married young. She identified their marital problems as stemming from her busy career. Margo came from a very traditional Italian-Catholic family. It was expected that the girls in the family would grow up to be stay-at-home moms and homemakers. This was exactly what Todd wanted in a wife and Margo, beautiful and sweet, fit the bill.

Early on, Margo's keen intellect had become obvious. She excelled in school and won many academic awards both in high school and college. During her senior year of college, a professor urged her to find a graduate program that would lead her to work in her field of interest.

To Margo's surprise, she was accepted at a prestigious graduate school. Todd was also surprised. He wasn't sure he liked this new ambition he saw in Margo. Margo remembers feeling that Todd was just indulging her: "He thought all this schooling was just a distraction until I was ready to get down to the business of having babies and staying at home."

In graduate school, Margo was soon engrossed in her studies and was busy going to classes and writing papers. She had little time left over for Todd. Margo promised him things would get better when her program was finished but Todd became increasingly enraged.

One night, Margo got home late from the library. As she stepped in their front door, Todd lunged for her, smacking her face and arms. Margo, too stunned to react, collapsed to the floor in tears. Todd immediately apologized. "He was so sorry and so contrite. He said that the stress of me not being available to him had put him over the edge. He cried. He couldn't believe what he had done. Neither could I."

Like most abusive partners, Todd promised it would never happen again. But it did. Feeling guilty about the move and her unavailability, Margo allowed the violence to continue.

"I was so overwhelmed with my workload, I really didn't have time to focus on what was going on at home," she explained. "I had never experienced domestic violence and thought it would all just go away once school was over and life got back to normal."

Once school ended, however, Margo was bombarded with impressive job offers. With Todd's reluctant blessing, she accepted a position that would allow them to move closer to their families.

When their first child was born, it became clear that Margo had no plans to stay home full-time with their new son. Todd felt duped by Margo whom he had assumed would stop working once she had children. The violence escalated. Margo and Todd briefly sought counseling but Todd warned Margo not to discuss the abuse in their sessions. Frightened of his outbursts, Margo complied.

Until she came into my office, Margo had never confided in anyone about the abuse. She was deeply ashamed of putting up with it for so many years. She refused to consider divorce because of her religious beliefs. She also believed her family would never condone a divorce. Believing otherwise, I advised Margo to go to her parents or sisters and explain her situation. When she did, her family immediately jumped into action, urging Margo to end the marriage. A short while later, Margo filed for divorce.

"I'm not sure why," Margo said, "but I ignored Todd's roughness at the beginning of the relationship. There was the occasional forceful grab of my arm or little shove during an argument. But I convinced myself the good in the relationship outweighed the bad. If anyone had told me ten years ago that I was going to get my doctorate, be abused by my husband and get divorced, I would've laughed in their face."

Because Margo is a strong, beautiful, highly-educated woman with a supportive family, she's a proof that domestic violence can happen to anyone. Margo wasn't weak or marginalized. Margo wasn't lonely or fragile. Margo was and is an interesting, smart, successful and admirable woman.

Many women ignore signs at the beginning of relationships that their partners may be physically abusive. More often than not, the more serious abuse doesn't start until after the couple is married. As with so many other things, women make the mistake of thinking that things will get better after marriage. Unfortunately, it's usually the more negative behaviors that become exacerbated.

If you think he's stressed about money now, if you think he's just tired or overworked, if you think he's overwhelmed with responsibilities and you're using these as excuses for physical violence…ding-ding-ding! That's your wake up call, sister. You ain't seen nothin' yet. You likely don't yet have the big mortgage, the newborn twins, the dual car payments, the ailing parents, or the you-name-it that pushes all of us to the brink at some point or another.

If you're unsure whether you're a victim of abuse, confide in a close friend or counselor. Abuse thrives in dark secrecy and bringing it out into the light can expose it for the nightmare it is. If your friend or counselor confirms your fears, it's time to decide whether you're going to sign up for a lifetime of physical abuse. If you think, "It's alright, I can handle some violence now and then," remember that a life involving physical abuse is *always* a life of secrecy, shame and pain. If that doesn't convince you, think about your children and what having this man in their lives will mean for them. Then decide.

Emotional (or Psychological) Abuse

I could have glommed this section onto the one about physical abuse but I feel strongly that it needs its own mention. Like physical abuse, emotional abuse thrives in the dark. Sometimes it's even harder to identify because it's so insidious and there are usually no outward signs. Often, women don't recognize their partners' behaviors as abusive until they get counseling or others start to notice changes in them.

Since it can take many forms, there isn't one easy way to define emotional abuse. One or more of the below experienced by the victim *on an ongoing basis* may indicate that emotional abuse is present in your relationship:

1) Feeling you must work perpetually to please your partner with little positive feedback from him.
2) Feeling you're a bad person or one deserving ongoing punishment.
3) Feeling anxious before you see your partner because you don't know what mood he will be in or if he will be angry at you for something intangible or a trivial infraction.
4) Feeling you need to constantly defend your actions, decisions, or whereabouts.
5) Feeling sad, depressed, anxious and helpless with respect to the relationship.

If you find yourself rationalizing or defending any of the factors on this list, that could also be a sign of emotional abuse. Of course, from time to time, you may feel sad about your relationship or your partner may be angry at you for valid reasons. I'm referring to a continuous experience of any one or more of the items on this list. I'm talking about your *perpetual feeling state*.

I know, I know. You're not perfect. Got it. Perhaps you've done something that really got under your man's skin. Maybe you lied to him about your credit report or kissed his best friend for a couple of seconds too long at last year's drunken New Year's party. You have some making up to do.

If your guy is going to emotionally abuse you, though, he's going to find a motive and run with it. A man who emotionally abuses his woman will always find a reason to do so. Then he will convince you that your behaviors are so egregious that he has no other choice than to deride and berate you on an ongoing basis.

Yes, this can happen to you. No, you're not better, stronger or smarter than the women it happens to every day. Sorry.

In any and every case, your man has a clear choice. He can work through your relationship struggles or he can leave the relationship. Simple as that. He does not get to stay in the relationship and punish and demean you for all eternity. He does not get to spend the next 50 years treating you like a second-class citizen and using your errors in judgment and your stumbles as vehicles to emotionally abuse you. Are you clear?

"Yes, Abby, I'm clear," I think I heard you say. Whew. I feel so much better now.

CHAPTER NINE

Theirs and Ours: Making Your Marriage Your Own

You'd be right if you said you're marrying your fiancé and not his family and friends. Technically, anyway. True, you're only exchanging vows with your guy. But you're also signing up to spend the rest of your life with the people he brings to the marriage with him.

Marriage is unique this way. Suddenly, you have a whole new family and a new gaggle of friends to manage. If your life had taken another turn, it's likely you never even would have met these folks. It's like being thrust onto the set of a strange soap opera; you don't know the story line so figuring out your place in this cast of characters can be a bit overwhelming.

I don't doubt that you could endure Thanksgiving dinner with the devil himself if you absolutely had to. But married life with your fiancé's family and friends is likely to involve more than some turkey and stuffing on a November afternoon once a year. They are your new relatives and, if you choose to have children, these folks will be those children's grandparents, aunts, uncles, cousins and godparents. On every holiday, special occasion, time of sadness, and a million moments in between, they will be at the center of your family's life.

The people your fiancé has chosen as his friends will tell you a lot about him. You may not be crazy about them but if they seem to be good, decent people, you're probably in good shape. If you can't stand their ethics and values, realize that this could spell trouble in your relationship if it hasn't already. We all know the adage about birds of a feather. Let's just say racists and civil rights advocates don't usually run in the same circles. You get the picture.

If you truly cannot bear to be in the presence of these folks, you need to figure out why and, if possible, how you can improve the situation especially if you want a marriage that's at least passably peaceful.

"Well, I tried to be nice," you may be thinking, "But they never welcomed me. They were rude to me from day one." Or you may be saying to yourself, "They're fine as long as I don't have to spend too much time with them. I'm hoping to curb our involvement with them as time passes."

Uh-oh.

A reminder in case you've forgotten: these people are your fiancé's family and chosen friends. Until he met you, they were the most important people in his life. This nagging, needy woman standing in front of you? She's his mother. She may not have been perfect but she did have a hand in raising the man you're now in love with. (You *are* in love with him, right? See Chapter One for review).

And that cantankerous older man in the other room? Meet his father, your fiancé's prototype for manhood. Don't like what you see? Telling yourself your fiancé will never be anything like that bigoted loudmouth with hair growing out of his ears? Think again.

In fact, take a good, hard look at his family while you still have the chance. These are the folks who reared him. Whether you're young enough to think the two of you won't turn out like your parents or old enough to know that's a crock of crack, know this: Everything he learned about relationships, he learned from them. He learned how adults manage household stress and shoulder family responsibility. He learned what it means to be a husband and father. Most importantly, he learned how love looks and feels.

Those lessons are what I call the old standards. They are the values both you and your fiancé gleaned from your families of origin. Maybe there's some really good stuff to be salvaged from those old standards but there's also likely a whole bunch of crap you'd like to put out with yesterday's trash. Now is the time for the two of you to tease out the old standards worth salvaging and launch the new standards for the marriage you want to build.

Hannah's story is perfectly illustrative of how parents' unhealthy communication patterns can create future relationship issues for their children.

Hannah is a pretty and lively 21-year-old college student who came to see me to discuss her relationship with her boyfriend, Rick. Hannah and Rick had met on a study abroad program which meant that once they returned back to the States, they would be living 500 miles apart on separate college campuses. Nonetheless, they decided they would endure the geographical separation and forge on with the relationship vowing to figure it out as they went along.

Almost immediately after returning home, Rick resumed contact with an ex-girlfriend. For some time, he told Hannah he "couldn't decide" which relationship he should be in. Hannah was heartbroken. All the promises he had made overseas seemed to be evaporating. Ultimately, Rick chose Hannah and their relationship resumed.

Hannah felt good that she and Rich had weathered that storm until rumors that he had been cheating on her began to enter her airspace. When Hannah confronted Rick, he confessed immediately. Hannah was impressed with his honesty. She took him back. This cycle repeated itself several times always ending with Rick making grand gestures to get back into her good graces. He would fly into town to surprise her or have flowers delivered to her classroom while her professor and dozens of her classmates looked on.

Hannah was confused as to why she was putting up with Rick's behaviors. As far as she knew, neither of her parents had ever had an affair. The thought was anathema in her rigidly religious family. She didn't understand why she would forgive Rick's repeated infidelities only to be wowed by his next flamboyant gesture of apology.

After some digging, Hannah realized that her father had often behaved badly in his marriage. Although he didn't have affairs, he was controlling and could be cruel to Hannah's mom and to his kids. After one of his "fits" he would buy her mom expensive jewelry or surprise Hannah and her siblings with a new puppy or unplanned vacation. Grandiose apologies were his specialty.

More times than she could count, Hannah observed her mother forgive her dad's outrageous behaviors. A pair of diamond earrings seemed enough to assuage the damage of the weeks of emotional pummeling her mom had endured. Hannah learned that bad behavior was always forgivable as long as the person apologized, preferably with impressive gestures. She was repeating that paradigm time and again with Rick.

Like Hannah, you and your fiancé unwittingly absorbed healthy and unhealthy ways of interacting from your parents. Think about what you learned about communication from them. If you can't objectively analyze what went on in your parents' marriages, start by telling stories about them. When did you see them happiest? What did they fight about? If one or both of their marriages didn't last, talk about why you think that was the case. Discuss what worked in their marriages. What things would you rather not duplicate your own marriage?

Part of this new vision may be defining or re-defining family role expectations. Do you and your fiancé share the same ideas about how the division of labor will look once you're married? Sad to say, but many a hip, urban guy morphs into his Ward Cleaver-like dad once the wedding bells have been rung. Up to this point, let's hope he's spent some part of his life doing his own laundry, washing his own dishes and cooking for himself. You may be quietly celebrating your luck in finding this chore-enlightened guy only to find that he's only done them thus far because he doesn't have a wife. Sound crazy? I promise you, it's not.

Take a look at yourself, too, sweetheart. Are you whipping up gourmet meals every night and lovingly pressing his shirts because even the dry cleaner's efforts aren't worthy of His Perfectness? If so, you're making unspoken promises to him that these things will continue throughout your marriage. He has no reason to believe they won't and the likelihood that you can or will keep them up is…how do they say it? Oh yes, slim to none.

Be honest with yourselves and negotiate now. Don't wait until you're sobbing and waist-deep in his dirty laundry to clarify how you feel. Don't set the expectation that you'll be whipping up *boeuf bourguignon* every night when you have three kids under four years old. Whether you make less money or more, choose to stay at home with the kids or not, work part-time or full, consider this: You are not getting married to have a boss, you're getting married to have a partner.

Don't assume (=ass/u/me) you're on the same page until you know you are. Together, create a vision list of ways you'd like chores to be divvied up when you're married. For example,

ABBY RODMAN, LICSW

your ideal may be to alternate cooking and cleaning up, bringing in the dry cleaning, and paying monthly bills. His vision may be different. Remember: this marriage thing is all about compromise. So, yes, you're going to have to do some of that.

Do the same for finances. Have the two of you created your own vision for how your money will be spent and/or saved? How will each of you access the money that you have? Will you combine your income and bills or keep them separate? How will household bills be paid?

Financial stressors and misunderstandings have shattered many a marriage. In fact, financial strain is always near the top of the list of reasons for marital discord. Talking about money can be uncomfortable. Perhaps you've been taught that it's too intimate a topic for discussion, or that bringing up dollars and cents is just plain crass. In some cases, that may be true. But if you can't do intimate or crass with your fiancé, who are you going to do it with? This is marriage, people. Any romantic hopes you may harbor will run quickly ashore when bill collectors come calling.

If your parents fought about money and you vowed you never would, remember this: *Your parents were fighting about money.* There was a reason for that. They disagreed on how money should be saved or spent. They fought about one or the other spending too much and on what. They fought because there wasn't enough or one couldn't account for where it all had gone. If you don't want to fight about money the way your parents did, don't. Do the work now and co-create your financial vision.

Discussing and creating a new vision of your impending marriage can be a fun and liberating exercise. Only the two of you can create this unique union and make it what you want it to be. Try to be as detailed as you can. Write it all down. Then, in the future, you can pull out your vision list and see how close you've come to achieving your ideal.

CHAPTER TEN

Answer This Question or Forever Hold Your Peace

My fiancé is: sweet, loving, moody, sexy, easily distracted, smart, insightful, defensive and protective. He would do anything for his friends. He loves his mom to pieces. He's very funny and generous to a fault.

When I ask him to do something for me, he always does it. On his time. He focuses on what's in front of him and not the bigger picture. These things annoy me. He has OCD tendencies. He works really hard to make me happy. He's a good father and a decent enough ex-husband. He's respectful of my religious and spiritual beliefs. He has a solid work ethic. He says stupid shit sometimes (really stupid shit example comment deleted here) and it pisses me off.

There is no one I'd rather be with or talk to. He is a great advice-giver. He still flirts with me. He's willing to make sacrifices and compromises on issues big and small. He doesn't roll his eyes when I have my tarot cards read. He encourages me to talk with my brilliant therapist when I'm struggling. He swears. A lot.

He drives me insane and makes me well. He's the first person I call when something happens. He's the first person I want to call. I can tell him anything and he doesn't judge me. When I complain about someone, his attitude immediately is, "That person sucks." I love that. He gets a little bummed out when I lose weight. I can't lie; I love that, too.

Yep. This is the guy for me. Not because he's perfect (not even close) but because his imperfections are okay with me. I know where he's coming from and where his head is at. I can manage his brand of difficult. There are no hidden agendas and no mind games. It's the good, the bad and the ugly front and center. That feels right.

During my first engagement, I would lock myself in my fiancé's bathroom, sit on the closed toilet seat and quietly sob. This didn't happen once, friends, it happened *all the time*. Incredible as it sounds now, it didn't occur to me then that this was a huge, honking, red relationship flag and that something was fundamentally wrong. I was young and hopeful. My family of origin was a relatively unhappy, dramatic place so these despairing feelings didn't feel so foreign to me.

I didn't know that I should have been asking myself some really hard questions. I didn't know that being swept off my feet didn't guarantee a happy marriage. I really, truly didn't know what (and who) I was getting myself into. I want something better for you. I want you to strip away all the goo and glitter and examine what's underneath. I want you to know your fiancé and your relationship as well as conceivably possible.

First and foremost, you need to be honest with yourself *about yourself* in this relationship. Start by answering these questions. In a conversation with a trusted friend, would you:

1) Describe honestly how you've felt in this relationship in the past week? Month? Year?

2) Edit any feelings or experiences you're ashamed or embarrassed about?

3) Omit any details about the relationship so as not to alarm or worry her?

4) Refuse to share any nagging doubts because you don't want to be talked out of getting married?

5) Be loathe to hear her concerns about the relationship knowing on some level that they may validate your own?

Think about your courtship. Has it been relatively easy or has it been fraught with tears and drama? Joining two lives is never a smooth road. You're merging your life with someone who comes with his own set of values, traditions, habits, and needs. You're learning to manage and accept his family and friends. These people may come to the table with their own visions for your relationship, another source of unneeded pressure.

Perhaps planning your wedding is already underway and it's been stressful in ways you didn't anticipate. Arguments have erupted and feelings have been hurt in the process. You've cried yourself to sleep a few times. You've complained to your friends about your fiancé's stubbornness and how outrageously difficult his mother can be. That's standard wedding-planning fare and if it's been manageable, grit your teeth and go ahead and make that nine millionth change to your seating plan.

Wedding aside, there may have been times throughout your relationship that your guy has pissed you off so much you've had second thoughts. Maybe you even took steps to end it at some point. Some of the things he does drive you nuts and you wonder if you can live with a guy who, say, views Monday Night Football with all the worship and awe due the Second Coming.

Maybe you've given in on points you never thought were negotiable. You always dreamed of living in the same neighborhood you grew up in and now you've agreed it'll be okay if you don't. Perhaps your cheaper-by-the-dozen dream of procreating has been negotiated and scaled back to a more realistic-by-the-pair. Hopefully, he's made concessions, too.

The endgame isn't perfection where perfection can't exist. The goal is respectful negotiation and compromise. In short, you win some and you lose some…and *so does he.* The endgame is the peaceful feeling you have when the two of you have reached an important decision together. Not because you'll always love the outcome but because of the manner in which that decision was reached. You've both been heard and your differing opinions lovingly considered.

I've always balked at the idea of happiness as a continual state of being. Happiness, I've found, is found in finite moments. That being said, you do know if something gives you an overriding feeling of comfort and contentedness. That's how I'm defining happiness for our purposes here. Conversely, you know what makes you uncomfortable or genuinely sad: a miserable job, living in a dangerous neighborhood, your friend's health concerns. Or perhaps a difficult, embattled relationship you probably shouldn't be considering for the long term.

That's why the ultimate question you need to ask yourself is this:

Am I happy in this relationship and with this person *most of the time?*

The answer to this question - be it yes or no - is life-altering and should be. Take a few hours, days or weeks and let it be your mantra: *Am I happy? Am I happy? Am I happy?*

Before you do anything else, you must get clear on this question. Does this relationship provide you with prevailing feelings of peace, safety and satisfaction? Are you able to look at the more difficult moments you've encountered with this man and feel assured that the two of you have resolved your differences respectfully?

Ask yourself this question until you're blue in the face,

until you're so sick of the word *happy* that it makes you want to vomit all over yourself. Ask yourself in the light of day and the darkest night. Ask yourself when you're talking to your man on the phone, when you're making love, when you're away from each other. Ask yourself after you've argued with him.

Ask yourself when he's being difficult or demanding or when you are. *Am I happy?* Ask yourself when that cute guy at work flirts with you. Ask yourself when a friend is glowing with reports of her own relationship. Ask yourself when your sister expresses her fear that your fiancé may not be the right guy for you.

Am I happy? Am I happy in this relationship, with this person, most of the time?

Answering yes doesn't mean every moment is wine and roses. It doesn't mean you're perpetually running through a field in a gauzy peasant dress with fresh flowers in your hair and a bluebird chirping on your shoulder. It means you have found a relationship that will bring you more peace than not. It means you've found someone who cherishes you and works hard for your happiness. This man will be by your side, a willing partner in the ongoing negotiations it takes to keep two people satisfied in a relationship. He puts you first and considers your opinion in all of his life's decisions.

Congratulations. I'm so pleased for you.

But what if the answer is a reluctant no? What if you realize, upon deep reflection, that you're not happy in this relationship with this man most of the time?

Perhaps there are moments of fleeting happiness and maybe he meets many of the standards you had for your future mate. But there's that nagging feeling that something—but what?—isn't quite right. Overt behaviors notwithstanding, only you can define the subtleties in your relationship that don't sit well with you. If you're plowing through the red relationship flags, you must ask yourself why you're so hell-bent on marrying this man.

Cara, an old acquaintance of mine, married her college sweetheart because, well, how could she not? Bright and attractive, they were the quintessential perfect couple. His family loved her and vice-versa. Victor, her fiancé, was a real catch. He was sweet, successful and clearly adored her. From the outside looking in, life appeared good for these two, no question.

Only problem was that on the day she got married, Cara was in the throes of a loving and passionate relationship with someone else. Confused and guilty, she walked down the aisle with a heavy heart. Only she knew the secret she was carrying.

A year into the marriage, and still in love with the other man, Cara divorced Victor. Cara and I fell out of touch after that and I never found out what had transpired in her ostensibly happy marriage. Years later, I ran into her and we had the chance to catch up a bit. By this point, she was publicly involved with the other man and was as happy as I had ever seen her.

"I really did care about Victor," Cara said, "We had been together so long and had been through so much. He was everything I thought I wanted in a mate and I just couldn't imagine calling off the wedding. Our families were so happy."

"If I'm completely honest, I think I married him because I just couldn't bear the idea of him being married to someone else. Selfish as it was, that's the reason," Cara said. "I married him knowing I didn't feel about him the way I should."

So, Cara was determined to marry Victor not because he was the right man for her but because she didn't want him to be the right man for someone else. She also didn't want to disappoint their families who had invested so much time and love into their relationship. Ending their engagement would have broken Victor's heart. Huge amounts of money spent on the wedding would never be recouped.

Cara is a beautiful, thoughtful, smart woman. She is no

dummy yet she married for all the wrong reasons and, in the process, hurt a lot of people, not least of all, herself.

If Cara had asked herself if she was truly happy in her relationship with Victor most of the time, the answer would clearly have been a difficult and painful no. As with many brides-to-be, Cara was on wedding autopilot. She thought things would resolve themselves after their nuptials. Newsflash redux: they rarely do.

"I'm deeply ashamed of what I did to Victor," Cara says, "It was such a sad and dark time for so many people and I created all of it. I walked down the aisle in a state of shock. I couldn't believe what I was doing. It was like I didn't even know myself anymore and what I did know, I didn't like."

Cara's point is a good one. If you have asked yourself whether you're happy in your relationship and can't quite figure out the answer, ask yourself another question: Do you like the person you are in the relationship? If you're not happy with who you've become with your fiancé, the union stands little chance of being a satisfying one.

Yes and alas, calling off an engagement is both complicated and agonizing. Some people will be angry and hurt and may distance themselves from you. The man you were about to join your life with will likely never speak to you again. Your family and friends may vacillate between support and disappointment. There will be accusations, blame, and tears. No matter how you slice it, it won't be pretty.

Here's what's less pretty. You get married knowing you probably shouldn't. You draw everyone you love into a day fraught with emotion and demanding economic investment. You lead everyone you love, including your fiancé, into believing you're making a lifelong commitment with a full and happy heart. You're deceiving everyone you love, most importantly yourself.

You're not a bad person. On the contrary! You feel you've led this parade of people who love you down this garden path of no return. How can you disappoint so many and turn back now? How can you forsake this man who has pledged his love and devotion to you? So you forge on.

Now, you're in an unhappy marriage. You see clearly all the signs you chose to disregard before you married this man. You stop wanting sex with him. You don't care whether you spend time together or not. All the quirky habits you took note of before you married him are now hugely offensive to you. Your friends and family start asking you what's wrong. "Nothing's wrong," you answer time and again - because you're too scared to admit that something is.

Eventually you admit to yourself that you've made a huge mistake. Perhaps you can disclose your misgivings to your husband and the two of you can seek counseling and try to improve things. Maybe you simply can't find the words and you act out by having an affair or distancing yourself emotionally from this man you promised to care for until death. He's hurt and confused. And so are you.

Months or years go by. Things only get worse. Your unhappiness trumps everything good in your life. You go to therapy and your therapist says, "So, you want me to tell you how to stay in a loveless marriage?" Your friends and family tire of your complaints and indecision.

Bravely, you make the decision to divorce. Hopefully, you haven't brought any children into this mess, but depending on how much time has gone by, it's conceivable that you have. If you thought telling folks you were breaking off your engagement was too tough, try sitting your parents down and telling them you're calling off your marriage. Try sitting your kids down and telling them.

You and your soon-to-be-ex start the divorce proceedings.

Except in highly unusual circumstances, you quickly realize there aren't enough assets for either of you to continue to live your lives as you had. You have to sell your house or get another job to make ends meet. Your kids are now and forever from a broken home. You struggle to coparent with a man who resents you. You'd like to date but you feel too wrecked, too tired even to begin to sort out what that might look and feel like.

Sound good so far?

Ladies, you need to wake up. You need to face with clarity the biggest decision you will ever have to make, the one decision that will have the greatest impact on your personal happiness for the rest of your life.

All relationships need to be tweaked now and then. Each of us has diagnosed ourselves with a physical or psychological disorder we've read about because finding hints of ourselves in any scenario is easy. If you've found traces of your relationship in this book, that doesn't mean your relationship is doomed. It could just mean that you and your fiancé need to make some adjustments, perhaps have some tough conversations you've colluded to avoid until now.

If, however, you've found more than traces of your relationship here, please pay attention. You are standing at the greatest crossroads of your life. Before you decide which way to turn, answer this question once again: "Am I happy in this relationship and with this man most of the time?"

Then, do what you need to do.

&

 Abby Rodman, LICSW, a psychotherapist in private practice, has counseled hundreds of individuals and couples with relationship issues. She has contributed articles to *The Huffington Post* and *The Boston Globe*. She is a featured relationship expert for yourtango.com. Abby is absurdly proud of her three amazing, college-aged sons who grew up at warp speed. Her next book in the Little Books for Life's Big Decisions series is about divorce and will be available in 2014. She lives outside Boston.

Find out more about the author and upcoming books online at www.abbyrodman.com or on Twitter at @abbyrodman

ACKNOWLEDGEMENTS

A million thanks (in no particular order) to:

- My smart, funny, sometimes exasperating, always adorable, and handsome-beyond-compare sons/PDs: "You'll never be able to say…"
- My mother, loving and beloved, for her never-faltering support
- My father, loving and beloved, for his advice, humor and writing expertise
- Lisa Tener, amazing book coach, for her encouragement and belief in my writing
- Adam Sexton, for his careful editing of this book and words of support
- Moriah Marston, therapist, lifesaver and seer extraordinaire
- Ted, ridiculously patient brother-in-law and book-titling connoisseur
- My extraordinarily wonderful friends, small in number but huge in devotion and love
- Ben Foster, loved and revered mentor. You are sorely missed.

A zillion thanks to:

- GMV, for confirming my lifelong belief that relationships like ours can and do exist…and, of course, for WTP. You will always have my heart.

An infinite number of thanks to:

- My beautiful, brilliant, and talented sister, Julie. This book (and my life) just wouldn't be complete without her.